THIS BOOK BELONGS TO

_____

GROWTH AND STUDY GUIDE

Loving God with All Your Mind

Elizabeth George

HARVEST HOUSE PUBLISHERS

EUGENE, OREGON

Cover by Dugan Design Group, Bloomington, Minnesota

Cover image © Antony Edwards/The Image Bank/Getty Images

Acknowledgment

As always, thank you to my dear husband, Jim George, M.Div.,Th.M., for your able assistance, guidance, suggestions, and loving encouragement on this project.

LOVING GOD WITH ALL YOUR MIND GROWTH AND STUDY GUIDE
Copyright © 1994 by Elizabeth George
Published by Harvest House Publishers
Eugene, Oregon 97402
www.harvesthousepublishers.com

ISBN-13: 978-0-7369-1383-6

ISBN-10: 0-7369-1383-1

Printed in the United States of America

11   12   13   14   / BP-KB /   13   12   11   10   9

CONTENTS

An Invitation to Love God Even More!. 7

1. Thinking on the Truth 9

2. Thinking the Truth About...God and His Word . . . 14

3. Thinking the Truth About...Others 19

4. Thinking the Truth About...the Future. 24

5. Thinking the Truth About...
   the Past and Present 29

6. Taking Every Thought Captive 34

7. Focusing on Today. 39

8. Scaling the Mountain of Today 44

9. Living One Day at a Time. 49

10. Living Out of God's Grace 54

11. Remembering to Forget 59

12. Finding the Gold 64

13. Going On and On and On 69

14. Focusing Forward...and Sailing On!. 74

15. Keep On Keeping On. 79

16. Pressing Toward God's Purpose 84

17. Trusting the Lord 89

18. Knowing God's Promise 94

19. Becoming Faith Oriented 99

20. Navigating the Maze of Life 104

21. Enduring Difficult Times 109

22. Bearing Fruit During Difficult Times 114

23. Becoming God's Masterpiece 119

24. Living Out God's Promise 124

25. Responding to Life's Turning Points 129

26. Majoring on the Minors 134

27. Trusting God in the Dark 139

28. Accepting the Unacceptable 144

Leading a Bible Study Discussion Group 149

An Invitation to

*L*OVE GOD EVEN MORE!

⟡

A Word of Welcome

Welcome to this helpful and practical handbook for you and others who yearn to love God—even more! I have revised the book *Loving God with All Your Mind* and updated and expanded the study questions to more effectively share six powerful promises from God that are truly life-changing! In fact, I've been told they are life-*saving!*

A Word of Instruction

The exercises in this study guide are easy to follow and to do. You'll need your copy of the revised edition of the book *Loving God with All Your Mind* (2005), your Bible, a dictionary, and a heart ready to change. In each lesson you'll be asked to read the corresponding chapter from *Loving God with All Your Mind* and to answer the questions designed to guide you to a deeper understanding of what it means to love God. By focusing on God and the truths found in His Word, the Bible, you'll become better equipped to handle your personal life issues and challenges.

A Word for Your Group

Of course, you can grow as you work your way through the biblical principles presented in this study guide and apply them to your life. But I urge you to share the rich and life-changing journey with others—with your friends, your neighbors, your Sunday school class, or Bible study. In a group, no matter how small or large, there is personal care and interest. There is sharing. There are sisters-in-Christ to pray for you. There is a mutual exchange of experiences. There is accountability. And, yes, there is peer pressure...which always helps us get our lessons done so that glorious growth occurs! There is sweet, sweet encouragement as you share God's Word with one another and stimulate one another to greater love and good works.

To aid the one who is guided by God to lead a group, I've included a section in the back of this growth and study guide entitled "Leading a Bible Study Discussion Group." You may also find this information and more on my website: **www.elizabethgeorge.com**.

A Word of Encouragement

If you will use the truths and the promises from God's Word that are spotlighted in the book *Loving God with All Your Mind* and in this exciting new study guide, by God's grace and with His help, you will begin to overcome the thoughts that overwhelm you with

    ❧ fear   ❧ worry

    ❧ depression   ❧ anxiety

    ❧ discouragement ❧ blaming

    ❧ bitterness   ❧ hopelessness

You—yes, you!—can know the inner joy and peace that comes from focusing your mind on what is true and good. The truths shared in this book will indeed positively transform your life...and the way you think, feel, and live!

In His everlasting love,

Elizabeth George

1

𝒯HINKING ON THE TRUTH

❦

 In *Loving God with All Your Mind,* read the chapter entitled "Thinking on the Truth." What meant the most to you from this chapter or helped you think more accurately about God's character and the truth of His Word?

What offered you the greatest challenge or blessing, and why?

Overcoming Depression

I shared my struggles with depression and my "dark days." Now it's your turn. What have you been struggling with in your personal life, either currently or at some time in the past?

God has the power to change us and the way we think. What "remarkable" progress have you made in gaining victory this week or at a previous time?

Turning to God's Word

I shared three practices God used to turn my life and daily struggles around. These disciplines centered around Philippians 4:8. Your problem is probably different from mine, but the methods for turning to and applying God's Word that follow on the next page can help you as well.

Memorizing God's Word—Write out Philippians 4:8 from your Bible here. Then write out your plan for memorizing it.

Meditating on God's Word—Meditating on Scripture involves asking questions about its meaning. For instance, think about how each of the eight "virtues" fits into the meaning of Philippians 4:8. Why is each one important? Which one is your favorite and why? Which do you admire most in others? Take a minute to answer any or all of these questions...or ask and answer your own questions. The most important thing in meditation is to *think*—to ponder—on the verse...and you can do that anywhere and at any time!

Applying God's Word—Regarding the application of God's Word, what is the message of James 1:22?

As you think about these three practices, what steps do you need to take?

Thinking on "These Things"

Look again at Philippians 4:8. What is the command in this verse? What boundaries does it place on your thoughts?

Breaking Through

Of the 10,000 thoughts that flow through your mind every day, how can thinking on the truth help with your thought life? What is a blessed result of following the advice of Philippians 4:8, according to verse 9?

Making Progress

"Whatsoever things are true...think on these things." Give an example from this past week of how the practice of these eight words corrected your "unhealthy thinking."

Realizing Strength for Daily Life

Hopefully the benefits of thinking on what is true and/or real are beginning to be evident. Share one instance when you realized God's strength for your daily life or for a trial because you chose to think on the truth.

What does Philippians 4:6-7 also advise for handling any problems?

Loving God...Even More

Read this section in your book again. As you consider the contents of this chapter and God's amazing love for you, what can you do this week, in obedience to Christ...

...to think on the truth?

...to train your thoughts?

...to love God with all your mind?

Think on these things.

$\mathcal{T}$HINKING THE TRUTH ABOUT...
GOD AND HIS WORD

In *Loving God with All Your Mind,* read the chapter entitled "Thinking the Truth About... God and His Word." What meant the most to you from this chapter or helped you think more accurately about God's character and the truth of His Word?

What offered you the greatest challenge or blessing, and why?

Thinking the Truth about God

Which of the following ideas or feelings do you regularly entertain?

— "I'm not really forgiven."

— "I must not be a Christian."

— "God doesn't know what's going on."

— "God doesn't see what's happening to me."

— "God doesn't understand how I feel."

— "God wouldn't do that for me."

— "God doesn't care about me."

— Other feelings or thoughts:

What truths do the verses below teach that contradict the ideas and feelings you marked above? How will you begin to change your thoughts so you are thinking the truth about God?

Exodus 2:24-25—

Exodus 3:7-10—

Genesis 16:7-14—

Genesis 21:17-19—

1 Peter 5:7—

Thinking the Truth about God's Word

Read 2 Timothy 3:16. What does this verse say about the value of God's Word?

Now, write out 1 John 1:9 from your Bible. What does this verse say about forgiveness?

Read Colossians 1:14. How does this verse give you additional assistance in thinking "forgiven"?

Redemption thru his Blood

Think the Truth about Ourselves

Read the following verses in your Bible. How can the truths of these verses help you replace the inaccurate ideas you sometimes have about God and yourself?

Psalm 139:14—

1 Corinthians 12:7-11—

Romans 5:8—

Romans 8:35—

2 Timothy 1:9—

Sometimes God's Word says one thing, and we think or feel differently. How should we view this contradiction and the power of God's Word to transform our thinking?

Loving God...Even More

Read this section in your book again. As you consider the contents of this chapter and God's amazing love for you, what can you do this week, in obedience to Christ...

...to think on the truth?

...to train your thoughts?

...to love God with all your mind?

Think on these things.

3

*T*HINKING THE TRUTH
ABOUT...OTHERS

❧

 In *Loving God with All Your Mind*, read the chapter entitled "Thinking the Truth About... Others." What meant the most to you from this chapter or helped you think more accurately about God's character and the truth of His Word?

What offered you the greatest challenge or blessing, and why?

Playing Mind Games

Mark any thoughts you regularly entertain about other people.

— "I don't think he/she means what he/she said."

— "I wonder what I've done wrong."

— "I wonder what he/she thinks about me."

— "I wonder what he/she wants from me."

— Other ways you second-guess people's motives or messages:

Understanding the Principle of Love

Read 1 Corinthians 13:4-8. What truths in these verses could help you with your nagging thoughts about what other people are thinking?

Putting the Principle of Love to Work

How will asking yourself "What is true?" help you stop second-guessing your relationships?

Understanding the Principle of a Clear Conscience

Read Matthew 18:15. How can obedience to this command assist you in your relationships?

discuss problem w/ friend

What is the similar command in James 4:17?

The greater the knowledge - the greater the accountability

If no one comes to you with a personal issue, what can you assume?

Putting the Principle of a Clear Conscience to Work

How does remembering the wisdom of Proverbs 28:1 help you proceed in your relationships?

Applying God's Principles to Your Thoughts

Consider what we've learned from Philippians 4:8 and what the guidelines "true" and "real" offer for your thoughts. What can you do, and what can God do to keep you from torturing yourself with unfounded (and, therefore, probably inaccurate) thoughts about what other people are thinking and feeling?

What will you do the next time you find yourself being suspicious, exaggerating, guessing, or making assumptions about someone's behavior?

How would your relationships improve if you accepted people's words at face value? Can you think of one specific instance where this would have helped?

Tapping into the Power of God's Word

Read Hebrews 4:12. How is the Word of God described?

What is God's Word able to do?

How does the Bible help you in your thought process?

What must you do to tap into this power?

Loving God...Even More

Read this section in your book again. As you consider the contents of this chapter and God's amazing love for you, what can you do this week, in obedience to Christ...

...to think on the truth?

...to train your thoughts?

...to love God with all your mind?

Think on these things.

4

$\mathcal{T}$HINKING THE TRUTH ABOUT…
THE FUTURE

In *Loving God with All Your Mind,* read the chapter entitled "Thinking the Truth About… the Future." What meant the most to you from this chapter or helped you think more accurately about God's character and the truth of His Word?

GOD is sufficient to be with us to handle any thing that comes along in the future.

What offered you the greatest challenge or blessing, and why?

The fact that I should leave the future to GOD & enjoy the present.

Crippling Fear

Check any fears you have, and put a star next to your greatest ones.

— Natural disaster

— Money/finances

— Marriage

— Children/grandchildren

— Singleness

✗ Widowhood

— Old age

— Illness/suffering

— Death

— Others:

How have these fears hindered you and your quality of life in the past? How are they inhibiting your life now?

My cancer doesn't go away dependatly — Insurance may not pick up treatments as I age —

Overcoming Fear

The Bible has much to say about not being fearful. What do these verses remind us about God's watch-care?

2 Timothy 1:7— *?*

Hebrews 13:6— *What can man do to us if GoD is with us?*

1 John 4:18— *Perfect love casts out fear —*

The following promises were given by God. Who were they given to, and what was the substance of the promise?

Genesis 15:1— *I am a shield for you. (Abram)*

Genesis 21:17-19— *Promise to Hagar + Ishmael*

Joshua 1:9— *Be strong & courageous Lord is with you —*

How can these promises help you overcome your fears?

Believe them,

Thinking about the Future

What is/are the "what if(s)" you think about most often?

Husband's death

What is true and real about your future? How can you remember these truths when you are tempted to be fearful?

GOD will be with me —

Asking "But What Is True and Real?"

Briefly note the truths the following Scriptures contain and how they apply to your specific fears about the future.

Joshua 1:9— GOD is with us

Psalm 23:1,4,6— Lord is my shepherd, I shall not want

Psalm 46:1-2— GOD is our refuge + strength

2 Corinthians 12:9— My grace is sufficient.

Philippians 4:13— I can do all things thru HIM who strengthens me

Philippians 4:19—

Hebrews 13:5-6—

What will you plan to do the next time you find yourself thinking, "What if…"?

Noting a Few "Nothings"

Review again the list of "nothings" in your book. Which one(s) encouraged you the most, and why? What can you add to the list?

Loving God...Even More

Read this section in your book again. As you consider the contents of this chapter and God's amazing love for you, what can you do this week, in obedience to Christ...

...to think on the truth?

...to train your thoughts?

...to love God with all your mind?

Think on these things.

5

$\mathscr{T}$HINKING THE TRUTH ABOUT...
THE PAST AND PRESENT

In *Loving God with All Your Mind,* read the chapter entitled "Thinking the Truth About... the Past and Present." What meant the most to you from this chapter or helped you think more accurately about God's character and the truth of His Word?

What offered you the greatest challenge or blessing, and why?

Thinking About the Past

What "if only" thought do you think most often?

How are your "if only" thoughts robbing you of a quality life in the present?

How has "if only" thinking been counterproductive in your life or the life of someone you know?

Remembering to Think on What Is True

According to the book, what two exceptions about your past are you to remember?

1.

2.

How does Psalm 77:11 remind you of how God brought you through a difficult time in your life?

What does Psalm 73:23-24 teach about God's presence in your past, in your present, and in your future?

Looking Back Through Eyes of Faith

What do the following Scriptures teach about your past?

Psalm 139:

Verse 13—

Verse 15—

Verse 16—

2 Corinthians 5:17—

Ephesians 1:4—

Ephesians 2:10—

2 Timothy 1:9—

What does Romans 8:28-29 state about your past?

What perspective on your personal history do Paul's words in Romans 8:28-29 give you?

Thinking About the Present

What disappointing,"but this isn't the way it was supposed to be" issue are you facing in your life today?

What does Philippians 4:8 teach you about your present situation?

Now, list several things you are going to do about "the way it really is."

Loving God...Even More

Read this section in your book again. As you consider the contents of this chapter and God's amazing love for you, what can you do this week, in obedience to Christ...

...to think on the truth?

...to train your thoughts?

...to love God with all your mind?

Think on these things.

6

$\mathcal{T}$AKING EVERY
THOUGHT CAPTIVE

❧

 In *Loving God with All Your Mind,* read the chapter entitled "Taking Every Thought Captive." What meant the most to you from this chapter or helped you think more accurately about God's character and the truth of His Word?

What offered you the greatest challenge or blessing, and why?

As I said in the book, I have been applying the following three steps to help train my thought patterns. May they assist you as well!

Step 1: Recognizing the Command

What is the command given to you in Philippians 4:8?

According to the verses below, what "resources" do you have to help you determine if some of the thoughts you are thinking are based on what is true and real?

Romans 9:1—

Hebrews 10:15-16—

2 Timothy 3:16-17—

Proverbs 12:15—

Step 2: Responding in Obedience

Consider Paul's words in 2 Corinthians 10:5. Share how each of the "resources" in the Scriptures that follow help you bring every thought captive to the obedience of Christ.

Romans 9:1—

Hebrews 10:15-16—

2 Timothy 3:16-17—

Proverbs 12:15—

Step 3: Reaping the Benefits

We have now completed the chapters about "thinking on the truth." Look again at the short list of benefits in your book. What benefits have you experienced thus far as you have been thinking on what is true and real?

Where have you seen the greatest growth in your Christian life? How has your life been more focused since thinking on what is true and real?

How has the reality of a "leaky bucket" affected your energy level in the past? Have you noticed any changes since you have been learning to think on what is true and real?

Loving God... Even More

Read this section in your book again. As you consider the contents of this chapter and God's amazing love for you, what can you do this week, in obedience to Christ...

...to think on the truth?

...to train your thoughts?

...to love God with all your mind?

Think on these things.

$\mathcal{F}$OCUSING ON TODAY

 In *Loving God with All Your Mind,* read the chapter entitled "Focusing on Today." What meant the most to you from this chapter or helped you think more accurately about God's character and the truth of His Word?

What offered you the greatest challenge or blessing, and why?

Looking at All of Life

Name the recurring issue or upcoming event in your life that is causing you the most anxiety today.

How can Psalm 118:24 encourage you today...and every day?

Looking at God's Word

In Matthew 6:34, what behavior does Jesus forbid?

How should Jesus' command affect the recurring issue or upcoming event you named above?

Looking at Today

Using your Bible, fill in Christ's formula for winning over worry found in Matthew 6:34.

His command—

His insight—

His challenge for you today—

Guideline 1: Prepare

Prepare in the evening—List the preparations you need to make tonight for what is most likely to happen tomorrow.

What do you think is the final step in preparing for tomorrow?

Prepare in the morning—Read Mark 1:21-34, and list the activities that filled a day in the life of Christ.

Now read Mark 1:35-38. After such a busy day, what was Christ's first activity the next morning?

By the time the first people reached Him, what had happened?

How would preparing in the morning help you when the day begins, reality sets in, and "everyone is looking for you"?

As you think about Christ's example, what steps will you take tomorrow morning that will allow you to receive the guidance, perspective, strength, and grace you need for the day?

As time allows, pray and then design your ideal devotional time.

The time:

The place:

The length of time:

The material and focus:

The role of prayer:

Loving God...Even More

Read this section in your book again. As you consider the contents of this chapter and God's amazing love for you, what can you do this week, in obedience to Christ...

...to focus on each day?

...to win over worry?

...to love God with all your mind?

Do not worry about tomorrow.

8

$\mathcal{S}$CALING THE MOUNTAIN
OF TODAY

In *Loving God with All Your Mind,* read the chapter entitled "Scaling the Mountain of Today." What meant the most to you from this chapter or helped you think more accurately about God's character and the truth of His Word?

What offered you the greatest challenge or blessing, and why?

Check any area(s) below that causes you anxiety or emotional stress.

— Finances	— Spouse
— Adult children	— Alcoholic spouse
— Teenagers	— Elderly parents
— Preteens	— Grandchildren
— Baby	— Job
— Moving	— Others:

What do you think causes people to worry about tomorrow? More specifically, why do *you* worry about tomorrow? What will you do to stop worrying and start following Christ's command in Matthew 6:34 to never be troubled about tomorrow?

What reason does Jesus give for not being anxious in Matthew 6:34?

Write out Matthew 6:34 on a 3" x 5" card. Carry this card with you for one week. Look at it every time you become anxious. By the end of the week try to say the verse from memory.

Guideline 1: Prepare

What mountains do you have to scale today? Check any areas below where you have responsibilities as a Christian woman.

— Wife

— Mother

— Daughter

— Employer/employee

— Other (list)

How can "preparing" relieve anxiety and worry in these areas of responsibility?

Guideline 2: Plan Ahead

Long-range planning—What long-range planning is needed in each area of responsibility?

Wife—

Mother—

Daughter—

Employer/employee—

Other (list)—

Short-term planning—What needs to go on today's "to-do" list in each of these areas?

Wife—

Mother—

Daughter—

Employer/employee—

Other (list)—

Guideline 3: Pray

Can you or did you commit to a prayer time each day for this week? Share briefly the time(s) you chose. Then list the three transactions that were suggested for your prayers:

1.

2.

3.

Guideline 4: Proceed

Share several ways you were blessed, or your anxiety level was reduced, by preparing, planning, and praying as you proceeded through your week.

Guideline 5: Trust God to Provide

How have you seen God provide as you have proceeded in faith this past week?

Loving God...Even More

Read this section in your book again. As you consider the contents of this chapter and God's amazing love for you, what can you do this week, in obedience to Christ...

...to focus on each day?

...to win over worry?

...to love God with all your mind?

Do not worry about tomorrow.

9

ℒIVING ONE DAY AT A TIME

In *Loving God with All Your Mind,* read the chapter entitled "Living One Day at a Time." What meant the most to you from this chapter or helped you think more accurately about God's character and the truth of His Word?

What offered you the greatest challenge or blessing, and why?

Read Matthew 6:25-34. What one word defines what this section of Jesus' Sermon on the Mount is about?

What basic needs in life does Jesus address, and what is His message and advice?

What did Jesus say about a person who worries (verse 30)?

The Living Bible translation of Matthew 6:34 says, "Don't be anxious about tomorrow. God will take care of your tomorrow too. Live one day at a time." According to this translation, how is an anxious-free person of faith to live his or her life? What does that mean to you?

Reviewing a Slice of History

I shared a little slice of my history and how, with God's help, I made it through an ordeal. I'm sure you've experienced a "slice of history," too. You may even be involved in an issue right now. Or you may know someone who is going through a tough time. In a sentence or two, review the difficult time here.

Look up these verses and describe the steps Jesus took on His difficult journey to the cross:

Mark 14:12-16—

Mark 14:22-25—

Mark 14:32-39—

Mark 14:40-42—

Managing Emotions

What is your present area of difficulty?

Now, work your way through the following steps, remembering how Jesus walked through His hour of difficulty. In a few words share how each step helps you manage the emotions life's difficulties can generate.

Step 1—Preparing

Step 2—Planning

Step 3—Praying

Step 4—Proceeding

Step 5—Trusting God

Loving God...Even More

Read this section in your book again. As you consider the contents of this chapter and God's amazing love for you, what can you do this week, in obedience to Christ...

...to focus on each day?

...to win over worry?

...to love God with all your mind?

Do not worry about tomorrow.

10

ℒIVING OUT OF GOD'S GRACE

✥

In *Loving God with All Your Mind,* read the chapter entitled "Living Out of God's Grace." What meant the most to you from this chapter or helped you think more accurately about God's character and the truth of His Word?

What offered you the greatest challenge or blessing, and why?

Learning More about Managing Emotions

Read these verses and describe some of the apostle Paul's emotions and physical challenges.

1 Corinthians 2:3—

2 Corinthians 1:8—

2 Corinthians 4:8-9—

2 Corinthians 7:5—

Managing Affliction

Read 2 Corinthians 11:23-28, and list some of Paul's physical afflictions induced by others.

Read 2 Corinthians 12:7-10. What was Paul's personal affliction in verse 7?

What was its purpose?

What did Paul ask God to do about it?

What was God's response?

What are some of the afflictions listed in verse 10 that Paul was prepared to endure?

What was Paul's response?

What physical challenges do you face, and how does 2 Corinthians 12:9-10 encourage you?

Look again at Matthew 6:34. What is Christ's command and the reason for it?

How can the command of Matthew 6:34 help you deal with...

...emotional stress and worry?

...concern about physical problems?

Read 2 Corinthians 10:5. Now, read the promises below. How can each assurance help you bring your anxious thoughts into obedience to Christ...even in the midst of emotional and physical stress?

Joshua 1:9—

1 Corinthians 10:13—

2 Corinthians 12:9—

James 1:5—

2 Peter 1:3—

Loving God...Even More

Read this section in your book again. As you consider the contents of this chapter and God's amazing love for you, what can you do this week, in obedience to Christ...

...to focus on each day?

...to win over worry?

...to love God with all your mind?

Do not worry about tomorrow.

$\mathcal{R}$EMEMBERING TO FORGET

In *Loving God with All Your Mind,* read the chapter entitled "Remembering to Forget." What meant the most to you from this chapter or helped you think more accurately about God's character and the truth of His Word?

What offered you the greatest challenge or blessing, and why?

Read Philippians 3:1-12. Even though Paul could have gloried in his past (verse 5-6), how did he choose to view it...

...in verse 7?

...in verse 8?

Why did he desire to reject the past (verse 7)?

What did Paul desire to gain instead in...

...verse 9

...verse 10

...verse 11

Read Philippians 3:12-14. Paul is saying, in effect, "I have not yet arrived at spiritual maturity and Christlikeness, but while I am on the way, I am conducting the journey by..." (verses 13-14)

_____ing

_____ing

_____ing

Forgetting the Past

Paul's goal was to press on. Look again at Philippians 3:13-14. What first step must you take in order to press on?

Share one success you have enjoyed in the past. What is Paul's advice to you, and why do you think remembering past achievements can be a detriment to pressing on for the prize?

By contrast, can you point to any past failure or flop that may be hampering your forward progress?

As you consider your answers to these questions, what changes do you need to make?

Forgetting the Bad

Read Acts 7:54-60. What part did Saul (Paul) play in the death of Stephen?

Read Acts 8:1-3 and Acts 22:4-5. What additional information do you learn about Paul's past?

In spite of a "bad" past, Paul moved forward in faith. How does his example encourage you as you look back at your past?

What comfort concerning your past do you find in the following scriptures?

—Psalm 103:12

—Isaiah 1:18

—Romans 8:2

—2 Corinthians 5:17

Loving God...Even More

Read this section in your book again. As you consider the contents of this chapter and God's amazing love for you, what can you do this week, in obedience to Christ...

...to press for the prize?

...to remember to forget?

...to love God with all your mind?

With the goal in view, I press on.

12

$\mathcal{F}$INDING THE GOLD

In *Loving God with All Your Mind,* read the chapter entitled "Finding the Gold." What meant the most to you from this chapter or helped you think more accurately about God's character and the truth of His Word?

What offered you the greatest challenge or blessing, and why?

Forgetting the Good

Read Philippians 3:4-6 again. What advantages and achievements did Paul enjoy?

What are some wonderful advantages and achievements God allowed you to experience before and after you became a Christian?

How can good things—advantages and achievements—keep you from growing as a Christian?

What perspective does Philippians 3:13-14 give you on the good things you listed above? Also note if there is anything you need to be actively forgetting.

Forgetting Success

Read 2 Corinthians 12:2-6. What was Paul's perspective on this most miraculous event?

Read Philippians 3:7-8 again. What does Paul's attitude teach you?

What past achievements or major accomplishment might be hindering your efforts to run the race? And what does Philippians 4:8—the charge to think on what is true and real—say to you about your past glories? What do you need to let go of from the past?

Three Steps for Forgetting

Is there any recurring memory of a bad or sinful thing from your past that continues to come to your mind and haunt you? Are you struggling in a bad situation now? If so, spend time praying about your past or the situation you are now facing. Then ask and answer these three questions:

Where is the gold?

Do I believe I am forgiven? Why or why not?

Who do I need to forgive?

Spend time thanking God for His abundant blessings in your life. Then ask God to show you where He would have you press on for Him. Jot down any decisions you need to make or steps you must take.

Loving God...Even More

Read this section in your book again. As you consider the contents of this chapter and God's amazing love for you, what can you do this week, in obedience to Christ...

...to press for the prize?

...to remember to forget?

...to love God with all your mind?

With the goal in view, I press on.

13

GOING ON AND ON AND ON

In *Loving God with All Your Mind,* read the chapter entitled "Going On and On and On." What meant the most to you from this chapter or helped you think more accurately about God's character and the truth of His Word?

What offered you the greatest challenge or blessing, and why?

Where Are You Going?

"Where am I going?" is the question a focused Christian would ask. It is a question regarding God's purpose. Read again the characteristics of a forward-moving, focused Christian. Which one of these characteristics do you need to work on? What first step can you take right away?

Where Is Your Focus?

Read the three checkup questions in the book on page 134. Which area of focus do you need to work on today? What first step can you take right away?

Paul knew the human tendency to rest, relax, and remember the past. Read Philippians 3:13-14 and 1 Corinthians 9:25-27 to see what Paul was doing to continue moving toward the goal he focused on. List the two or three that mean the most to you.

Focusing on the Present

Read Hebrews 12:1-2. Verse 1 mentions the weight and sin that keep people from reaching forward toward God. What are some activities or interests that keep you from running a better race?

Verse 2 mentions looking to Jesus. What changes in your mental attitude and focus would help you pursue God's purpose with more passion and concentration?

Can you say that all of your effort and energy is focused on God? What would make this statement more true of you?

Recognizing God's Purpose for You

How would you answer these questions?

Who am I?

Where did I come from?

Why am I here?

Where am I going?

Look at Philippians 3:12 in your Bible, then read this paraphrase: "I don't mean to say I am perfect. I haven't learned all I should even yet, but I keep working toward that day when I will *finally* be all that Christ saved me for and wants me to be" (TLB). As you review your answers above and Paul's statement in Philippians 3:12, do you think your focus is in the right place? What adjustments need to be made?

Loving God...Even More

Read this section in your book again. As you consider the contents of this chapter and God's amazing love for you, what can you do this week, in obedience to Christ...

...to press for the prize?

...to remember to forget?

...to love God with all your mind?

With the goal in view, I press on.

14

ℱOCUSING FORWARD...AND SAILING ON!

❧

In *Loving God with All Your Mind*, read the chapter entitled "Focusing Forward...and Sailing On!" What meant the most to you from this chapter or helped you think more accurately about God's character and the truth of His Word?

What offered you the greatest challenge or blessing, and why?

Pursuing Excellence

Read again the brief summary of Joseph's life in your book. (Even better, if you have the time, read Genesis 39–45.) Note how Joseph accepted and handled each of these difficult instances:

Sold into slavery by envious brothers (Genesis 39:1-6)—

Unjustly accused by Potiphar's wife (Genesis 39:6-23)—

Forgotten in prison (Genesis 40:1–41:1)—

What adversities or difficulties are you presently facing? How can you follow Joseph's example and "turn adversity into opportunity"?

Bearing Fruit in the Land of Your Affliction

Where has God placed—or "planted"—you, and how does Joseph's story inspire you to "bloom where you are planted"?

Existing...or Serving?

What model did Jesus set for us in Matthew 20:28? How far did He go to live out His purpose? Do you think Jesus was existing...or serving? Please explain your answer.

And how about you? Are you existing...or serving? Are you a Joseph, or would you be more like "the lady by the lake"? Please explain.

How would fresh goals focused on serving others help you be more active and productive in reaching and pressing for the prize found in Philippians 3:14? Can you name one new goal?

Fixing Your Heart and Mind on God

How do these scriptures help you fix your heart and mind on God?

Isaiah 26:3—

Philippians 4:6-7—

Keeping a Vigilant, Steady Focus

How has learning about forgetting, reaching, and pressing forward prepared you for handling stressful situations? Share a time when you chose to go on in spite of a stressful situation.

Hearing God's Voice

List a few reasons you think Christians fail to press for the prize of the upward calling of God in Christ Jesus. What is the greatest roadblock to your continuing efforts to press forward, and how can you overcome it?

Loving God...Even More

Read this section in your book again. As you consider the contents of this chapter and God's amazing love for you, what can you do this week, in obedience to Christ...

...to press for the prize?

...to remember to forget?

...to love God with all your mind?

With the goal in view, I press on.

15

$\mathcal{K}$EEP ON KEEPING ON

 In *Loving God with All Your Mind,* read the chapter entitled "Keep On Keeping On." What meant the most to you from this chapter or helped you think more accurately about God's character and the truth of His Word?

What offered you the greatest challenge or blessing, and why?

Our Call to Press On

Before we move on to the third step in Paul's pursuit of spiritual maturity, review Philippians 3:13-14 and list Steps 1 and 2:

Step 1:

Step 2:

What is Paul's third step for spiritual growth?

Would you describe your efforts at pressing on as giving your utmost for God's highest? Why or why not?

A Grand Purpose

Read Psalm 37:4-5. What is your part or role in these verses?

What is God's part or role in these verses?

How can you make sure you are doing your part?

What are your lifetime goals or desires? In very few words, jot down two or three of them.

A Concerted Effort

One of my daily desires is to live a purposeful lifestyle—to give my best and my all in everything I do. How do you think a "grand purpose" and lifetime goals encourage you to live a more purposeful lifestyle?

"Wings Like Eagles"

Read Isaiah 40:28-31. What is your part or role in these verses?

What is God's part or role in these verses?

How can you make sure you are doing your part?

Focusing on the Goal

Read Proverbs 3:5-6. What is your part or role in these verses?

What is God's part or role in these verses?

How can you make sure you are doing your part?

What are the desires of your heart...or, put another way, what are your lifetime goals?

Loving God...Even More

Read this section in your book again. As you consider the contents of this chapter and God's amazing love for you, what can you do this week, in obedience to Christ...

...to press for the prize?

...to remember to forget?

...to love God with all your mind?

With the goal in view, I press on.

$\mathcal{P}$RESSING TOWARD
GOD'S PURPOSE

In *Loving God with All Your Mind,* read the chapter entitled "Pressing Toward God's Purpose." What meant the most to you from this chapter or helped you think more accurately about God's character and the truth of His Word?

What offered you the greatest challenge or blessing, and why?

People in the Bible Who Focused to the End

In one sentence, what do you find most striking about the following individuals who pressed toward the finish in their journey of faith? Star the one that gives you encouragement or direction for this week.

Abraham (Hebrews 11:8-16,39)—

Moses (Numbers 27:12-23; Deuteronomy 31:7-8)—

Samuel (1 Samuel 8:1-5; 12:1,23)—

David (1 Chronicles 17:1-4; 22:5,8-11)—

Paul (Ephesians 6:19-20; Philippians 1:13;
    Philemon 1,9)—

John (Revelation 1:9,19)—

Christ (Luke 9:51; John 19:30; Hebrews 12:2)—

People in Our Time Who Focused to the End

Name a few people you know or know of who focused on giving their all for Christ to the end. What impressed you most about them?

Running Unencumbered

Read Hebrews 12:1. What habits, thought patterns, goals, or activities are holding you back, slowing you down, or keeping the pursuit of God from being the most important activity in your life?

What do you need to lay aside so that you can better serve God, so that you can be in better running condition?

A Look in the Mirror

Look one last time at Philippians 3:13-14. Paul's "one thing I do" was pressing toward the prize. Then look at Hebrews 12:1-4 (NASB). Note the verbs in each of the following phrases and share something you must do immediately.

"*Lay aside* every encumbrance, and the sin which so easily entangles us..."

"*Run* with endurance the race that is set before us..."

"*Fixing* our eyes on Jesus..."

"*Consider* Him...so that you will not grow weary and lose heart..."

Loving God...Even More

Read this section in your book again. As you consider the contents of this chapter and God's amazing love for you, what can you do this week, in obedience to Christ...

...to press for the prize?

...to remember to forget?

...to love God with all your mind?

With the goal in view, I press on.

17

𝒯RUSTING THE LORD

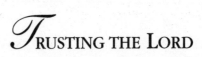

In *Loving God with All Your Mind,* read the chapter entitled "Trusting the Lord." What meant the most to you from this chapter or helped you think more accurately about God's character and the truth of His Word?

What offered you the greatest challenge or blessing, and why?

Knowing God

Write out Romans 8:28.

What truths about God are proclaimed in this verse?

For whom does God promise to work all things for good?

How should the truth about God and His promise in Romans 8:28 change your perspective and attitude toward your difficulties, losses, hurts, and tragedies?

Knowing God the Father

Read Matthew 6:9-13. To whom are you to pray?

How does this prayer show love toward God, respect for God, and dependence on God?

How does this prayer help you understand the Father's ability to take care of "all things" in your life and comfort you?

Knowing God Is at Work

What do the following verses say about God's work in your life?

Psalm 57:2—

Psalm 138:8a—

Philippians 1:6—

Philippians 2:13—

James 1:2-4—

Knowing God Works All Things Together

Look again at Romans 8:28. What does God want you to "know"—not hope or wish?

What does "all things" include? What are you struggling with most today?

If God promises to work all things together for good, how should that change your view on any bad things?

Loving God...Even More

Read this section in your book again. As you consider the contents of this chapter and God's amazing love for you, what can you do this week, in obedience to Christ...

...to count on God's goodness?

...to remember God's power at work in your life?

...to love God with all your mind?

We know that in everything God works for good.

18

$\mathcal{K}$NOWING GOD'S PROMISE

cs∞

In *Loving God with All Your Mind,* read the chapter entitled "Knowing God's Promise." What meant the most to you from this chapter or helped you think more accurately about God's character and the truth of His Word?

What offered you the greatest challenge or blessing, and why?

Knowing God Uses All Things

Fill in this blank: "My Number One problem is

_____."

How does the truth of Romans 8:28 encourage you with your Number One problem?

Name a good thing that has or is happening to you. A new job? A move? A new baby? A promotion at work? Retirement? How is God using this for good even though it comes with some tension and stretching?

Name a bad thing that has or is happening to you. What will you do to remember that God is using this for your good and His purposes?

How does knowing that in God's hands the end result will be good cause you to view the large (and sometimes bad) things that happen in life?

How do small things—such as insults, lost items, inconveniences, traffic jams—fit into God's plan to work all things for good?

Who are the people—bad and good, pleasant and difficult—God is using in your life for your good and His purposes? Pray for each one by name, and thank God for that person's part in fulfilling God's purpose in your life.

Knowing God's Promise

How can the truth of Romans 8:28 help you resist the negative responses that so often surface as a result of a difficulty, tragedy, rejection, or defeat, such as:

—doubt

—emotion

—bitterness

—other negative responses

—manipulation

Now read Romans 8:29. What is God's main purpose for your life and for all that He allows to touch your life? How does this encourage you in your problem issues?

Loving God...Even More

Read this section in your book again. As you consider the contents of this chapter and God's amazing love for you, what can you do this week, in obedience to Christ...

...to count on God's goodness?

...to remember God's power at work in your life?

...to love God with all your mind?

We know that in everything God works for good.

19

ℬECOMING FAITH ORIENTED

❧

In *Loving God with All Your Mind,* read the chapter entitled "Becoming Faith Oriented." What meant the most to you from this chapter or helped you think more accurately about God's character and the truth of His Word?

What offered you the greatest challenge or blessing, and why?

Read Ney's prayer again. What does her prayer teach you about being a woman who is "faith oriented"?

Praying God's Word

What difficulty, heartache, or tragedy are you in the midst of today? Have you filled in the blank and prayed the following? "Lord, Your Word says that all things—including _____—work together for good. Therefore, I choose to thank You." If you haven't, why not do so right now?

How can praying God's Word, rather than praying your own words (as sincere as they may be) contribute to making you a faith-oriented person?

Trusting God's Good Purpose

Joseph suffered greatly at the hands of his brothers. When he later faced them, what was Joseph's perspective and conclusion (Genesis 50:20)?

Are you facing a current trial or one that has been lingering in your life for some time? How do the truths of Romans 8:28 fine-tune your perspective and attitude toward your difficulties?

"Why is God doing this?" "Why is this happening to me?" Are these the kinds of questions you ask of the twists and turns of your life? If so, who is the focus in these questions?

What happens when you rephrase your question to, "What does this mean to *God?* What is it that *God* is wanting me to learn from this situation?" How does this change your perspective toward what is happening?

What does Matthew 7:9-11 teach about God, His goodness, and His good purposes?

Giving God Our Love

Again, to and for whom does God promise to work all things together for good?

———

———

What are some specific ways you can show your love for God, according to these scriptures?

John 14:15—

1 John 2:15—

1 John 4:20-21—

Does one of these areas in your life need improvement? What will you do about it this week?

Loving God…Even More

Read this section in your book again. As you consider the contents of this chapter and God's amazing love for you, what can you do this week, in obedience to Christ...

…to count on God's goodness?

…to remember God's power at work in your life?

…to love God with all your mind?

We know that in everything God works for good.

20

$\mathcal{N}$AVIGATING
THE MAZE OF LIFE

❦

 In *Loving God with All Your Mind,* read the chapter entitled "Navigating the Maze of Life." What meant the most to you from this chapter or helped you think more accurately about God's character and the truth of His Word?

What offered you the greatest challenge or blessing, and why?

Discovering God's Purpose

Fill in the last few words of Romans 8:28: "We know that all things work together for good to those who love God...

Read Romans 8:29. What does Paul say is God's main purpose for your life?

While you have been reading *Loving God with All Your Mind,* how have you seen God's promise and purpose (as stated in Romans 8:29) at work in your life? Share one instance.

Finding God's Will

Read Acts 16:6-10. Going through each verse, chart Paul's experience in "the maze of God's will."

—Verse 6

—Verse 7

—Verse 8

—Verse 9

—Verse 10

How and by what means did God guide Paul to ultimately realize God's will?

Discovering God's Purpose...for You!

Using the following questions, share how God has revealed His will to you.

Who are or were some of the people God has used?

What unusual events and/or circumstances has God used?

What were some things you wanted that God did not permit?

When and how has God stopped your movement in one direction and turned you another direction?

What do you see about God's will as you look back at your answers? What hope do you have for the future?

God's Songbird

How has God turned a negative event in your life into a blessing for you?

Loving God...Even More

Read this section in your book again. As you consider the contents of this chapter and God's amazing love for you, what can you do this week, in obedience to Christ...

...to count on God's goodness?

...to remember God's power at work in your life?

...to love God with all your mind?

We know that in everything God works for good.

$\mathcal{E}$NDURING DIFFICULT TIMES

In *Loving God with All Your Mind,* read the chapter entitled "Enduring Difficult Times." What meant the most to you from this chapter or helped you think more accurately about God's character and the truth of His Word?

What offered you the greatest challenge or blessing, and why?

God Has a Plan for You

Read Jeremiah: 29:1-11.

According to verse 4, who caused the captivity of the Israelites?

What advice does God give the exiles in verses 5-7 for how to live in a strange land?

What words of hope does God speak in verses 10-14?

What circumstances in your life does God seem to be asking you to live with and endure?

How does the knowledge of God's plan and purpose for you encourage you?

A—Acknowledge God's Hand

Look at Jeremiah 29, verses 4, 7, 14, and 20. Who does God
say was instrumental in the Israelites' captivity?

What differences does acknowledging God's hand in your situation make?

B—Bloom Where You Are Planted

Read Jeremiah 29:5-7. What did God say to His people
about putting down roots and getting busy in their captivity?
List the involvement He expected.

What difference do you think such activities make in difficult
times?

Where has God "planted" you? How have you acknowl-
edged His hand, and what are you doing to "bloom" there?

C—Count on God's Promises

What was God's promise to Israel in Jeremiah 29:10 and 14?

What are just a few of God's promises to you?

John 10:27-29—

John 14:1-3—

Philippians 1:6—

1 Thessalonians 4:16-17—

D—Do Something Useful

What is Matthew 20:26-28 calling us to do?

What guidelines does God give for serving...

as a wife in Genesis 2:18?

as a mother in Titus 2:4?

as an employee in 1 Peter 2:18?

as a member of the body of Christ in Galatians 6:10?

as a witness to Him in the world in 1 Peter 3:15?

As you review these four ABC's, what message is God sending to you in your difficult situation?

Loving God...Even More

Read this section in your book again. As you consider the contents of this chapter and God's amazing love for you, what can you do this week, in obedience to Christ...

...to live out God's plan?

...to trust God's promise?

...to love God with all your mind?

God has a destiny and a hope for you.

$\mathcal{B}$EARING FRUIT DURING DIFFICULT TIMES

❦

In *Loving God with All Your Mind,* read the chapter entitled "Bearing Fruit During Difficult Times." What meant the most to you from this chapter or helped you to think more accurately about God's character and the truth of His Word?

What offered you the greatest challenge or blessing, and why?

Learning from God's Servants

What messages do these saints offer you as you consider their usefulness in spite of difficult times?

Joseph (Genesis 39:4,22; 41:56)—

Paul (2 Corinthians 11:23-28)—

What messages do these more modern-day saints offer you about bearing fruit during difficult times?

Madame Guyon—

Mrs. Studd—

Hudson Taylor—

Doing God's Will

"What is God's will for my life?" Read Psalm 37:4, and walk through these suggested steps for discovering God's will.

1. *Delight yourself in God*—What does "delight yourself" mean with respect to your relationship with God?

   What is God's promise?

   What is the condition for participating in this promise from God?

2. *Indulge yourself in God's Word*—What image comes to your mind when you hear the word "indulge"?

   How would you measure your interest in God's Word at this time? Do you need to make any changes?

3. *Committing yourself to the Lord*—Read Psalm 37:5.

What are you to commit to God?

What else does God ask of you?

What is God's promise to those committed to His ways?

God declares that He has a plan for you. List what you can do to help your plans match God's plans as stated in…

Proverbs 3:5-6

Proverbs 16:3

Based on your list, what specific changes or activities will ensure that you further delight yourself in the Lord and commit yourself to Him?

Loving God...Even More

Read this section in your book again. As you consider the contents of this chapter and God's amazing love for you, what can you do this week, in obedience to Christ...

...to live out God's plan?

...to trust God's promise?

...to love God with all your mind?

God has a destiny and a hope for you.

$\mathcal{B}$ECOMING GOD'S
MASTERPIECE

In *Loving God with All Your Mind,* read the chapter entitled "Becoming God's Masterpiece." What meant the most to you from this chapter or helped you think more accurately about God's character and the truth of His Word?

What offered you the greatest challenge or blessing, and why?

Learning to Look at God's Good Plan

When life is difficult, it's easy to doubt God, wonder about His goodness, and question His wisdom. The Israelites faced 70 years of exile in a foreign land.

If you had been one of the Israelites, what would your thoughts have been?

Identify again the difficulties you are currently enduring.

What thoughts do these hard times sometimes tempt you to think?

God's Good Plan is an Adventure

What do these scriptures teach about God's good ways, and how does each one encourage you?

Jeremiah 29:11—

Romans 8:28—

Romans 8:32—

James 1:13—

1 Peter 5:10—

God's Good Plan Is a Process

Sometimes Christians are tempted to think that God has planned something ugly for them, or that He is making a mess of their lives. How does the promise of Jeremiah 29:11 correct these thoughts that are not true?

As you consider your present difficult situation, what do you see thus far in God's process that you can be thankful for?

God's Good Plan Is an Opportunity

List several ways spiritual and personal growth occurs as you treat adversity as an opportunity.

What do these verses add to your list?

    2 Corinthians 1:3-4—

    James 1:2-4—

    1 Peter 5:10—

Loving God...Even More

Read this section in your book again. As you consider the contents of this chapter and God's amazing love for you, what can you do this week, in obedience to Christ...

...to live out God's plan?

...to trust God's promise?

...to love God with all your mind?

God has a destiny and a hope for you.

24

ℒIVING OUT GOD'S PROMISE

⚬◈⚬

In *Loving God with All Your Mind,* read the chapter entitled "Living Out God's Promise." What meant the most to you from this chapter or helped you think more accurately about God's character and the truth of His Word?

What offered you the greatest challenge or blessing, and why?

God's Good Plan: Purging and Pruning

What benefits does pruning promote in the growth of plants?

What benefits does pruning promote when it comes to your spiritual growth?

How did "pruning and purging" promote God's good plan for the apostle Paul, as seen in 2 Corinthians 12:6-10?

How did God say His process would benefit believers in 1 Peter 1:6-7?

Are there any areas you have been reluctant to yield to God for purging and pruning? Pray now to give them over to God. Let the growth process begin!

God's Good Nature

Look again at the *four* scriptures written out in this section in the book. Then look in your Bible at these *three* additional references. Note what they reveal about God's goodness, and jot down the words and phrases that especially minister to you.

—Psalm 23:1,6

—Psalm 84:11-12

—Romans 8:28

How can you remember God's promise that His plan is for your good?

Write out a prayer using the words and phrases from the *seven* verses referred to in this section as a reminder of God's goodness and His care for you.

Looking to the Reward

How does the promise of Jeremiah 29:11 *rebuke* you when you doubt the process God is taking you through?

How does the promise of Jeremiah 29:11 *comfort* you when you feel hopeless or depressed?

How does Jeremiah 29:11 *encourage* you as you wait for God's promised and "expected end"?

Regardless of how you may "feel," what are God's plans for you, according to His promise in Jeremiah 29:11? Now, how does that make you feel?

How does God's promise in Jeremiah 29:11 help you stay positive in the midst of hard or trying times?

Loving God...Even More

Read this section in your book again. As you consider the contents of this chapter and God's amazing love for you, what can you do this week, in obedience to Christ...

...to live out God's plan?

...to trust God's promise?

...to love God with all your mind?

God has a destiny and a hope for you.

25

$\mathcal{R}$ESPONDING TO LIFE'S TURNING POINTS

⁓⬳⬲⁓

 In *Loving God with All Your Mind,* read the chapter entitled "Responding to Life's Turning Points." What meant the most to you from this chapter or helped you think more accurately about God's character and the truth of His Word?

What offered you the greatest challenge or blessing, and why?

Turning Points

Can you think of any "turning points" in your life? What happened, and how has your life changed as a result?

Accepting God's Will

Read Luke 1:26-38. Describe Mary's turning point.

Why did God choose to use Mary's life in this way?

What was Mary's one-and-only question?

How did the angel Gabriel ultimately answer Mary's question and address the miracle of Elizabeth's pregnancy?

How did Mary indicate her acceptance of God's will for her life?

The Mentality of a Handmaiden

Write out Mary's reply to Gabriel's announcement in verse 38.

What impresses you most about it?

Describe the role and attitude of a handmaiden as pictured in Psalm 123:2.

Is yours the heart and mind of a handmaiden? Have you ever uttered something like Mary's incredible words of acceptance in Luke 1:38 when a turning point arrived? Why or why not?

A Knowledge of God

Read Luke 1:46-55, and list some of the facts about God that Mary articulated.

To learn even more about the person and character of God, read Hannah's prayer in 1 Samuel 2:1-10. List some additional facts about God that Hannah expressed.

How does Mary's knowledge of God speak to you and your own mysterious life situations?

The Depth of the Riches of God

Read Romans 11:33-36. List some of the facts about "the riches of God" contained in Paul's glorious "doxology."

Loving God...Even More

Read this section in your book again. As you consider the contents of this chapter and God's amazing love for you, what can you do this week, in obedience to Christ...

...to think on the truth about God?

...to trust God "in the dark"?

...to love God with all your mind?

Oh what a wonderful God we have!

26

$\mathcal{M}$AJORING ON THE MINORS

 In *Loving God with All Your Mind*, read the chapter entitled "Majoring on the Minors." What meant the most to you from this chapter or helped you think more accurately about God's character and the truth of His Word?

What offered you the greatest challenge or blessing, and why?

Focusing on God

Read Romans 11:33 in a different translation than you normally use. How does God's Word describe these "majors" about God: His wisdom, knowledge, judgments, and ways?

Using a dictionary, give simple definitions for the following words:

unsearchable

unfathomable

inexhaustible

inscrutable

impossible

In five to ten words, describe these terms as a whole.

Acknowledging the Wisdom of God

When you need wisdom, where or to whom do you generally go?

What do these scriptures say about wisdom?

   —Proverbs 2:6

   —Proverbs 9:10

   —James 1:5

What do you normally do when you run up against something in the Bible that you don't agree with or understand? How does God's wisdom call you to exercise your faith in Him?

Acknowledging the Knowledge of God

Read Psalm 139. According to the psalmist, what does God know about you as revealed in these verses?

—Verse 1

—Verse 2

—Verse 3

—Verse 4

—Verse 13 (When?)

—Verse 15 (When?)

—Verse 16 (When?)

—Verse 23

What does the psalmist say in verse 6 about God's knowledge?

Realizing God Knows All About Us

Reflect on the truth that God knows all the details of your life. How does the fact of God's knowledge enable you to accept your circumstances?

Loving God...Even More

Read this section in your book again. As you consider the contents of this chapter and God's amazing love for you, what can you do this week, in obedience to Christ...

...to think on the truth about God?

...to trust God "in the dark"?

...to love God with all your mind?

Oh what a wonderful God we have!

$\mathcal{T}$RUSTING GOD IN THE DARK

 In *Loving God with All Your Mind,* read the chapter entitled "Trusting God in the Dark." What meant the most to you from this chapter or helped you think more accurately about God's character and the truth of His Word?

What offered you the greatest challenge or blessing, and why?

Remembering God's Wisdom and Knowledge

Look at your dictionary definitions on page 135. Copy below your 5-10 word summary of the terms unsearchable, unfathomable, inexhaustible, inscrutable, and impossible.

Here are a few things God knows about you:

- God *knows* every situation in your life.

- God knows *why* each situation is in your life.

- God knows *how* each situation will end.

- God knows *when* each situation will end.

How does the truth that God knows all about you enable you to better accept the unacceptable, difficult, and painful situations of your life?

Acknowledging God's Judgments

Read Psalm 19:9-11. How are God's judgments character-
ized in verse 9?

—

—

What two desirable things described in verses 9-10 are less
desirable than God's judgments?

—

—

What is the result of heeding God's judgments (verse 11)?

—

Read Psalm 119:137. How is God's judgment described?

Read 119:1-8. List some of the other words used inter-
changeably with God's judgment.

Accepting without Answers

When the angel Gabriel told Mary that she would bear God's Son, she accepted something she did not understand. What do you think keeps you or others from responding to the un-understandable events of life with Mary's accepting attitude, "Behold the maidservant of the Lord! Let it be to me according to your word" (Luke 1:38)?

Acknowledging God's Ways

God's ways are the methods by which He carries out His judgments. What do you learn about God's ways in Isaiah 55:8-9?

How does the fact that God's ways are unsearchable and unfathomable help you to "trust God in the dark" in your difficult situation?

Loving God...Even More

Read this section in your book again. As you consider the contents of this chapter and God's amazing love for you, what can you do this week, in obedience to Christ...

...to think on the truth about God?

...to trust God "in the dark"?

...to love God with all your mind?

Oh what a wonderful God we have!

28

$\mathcal{A}$CCEPTING THE UNACCEPTABLE

In *Loving God with All Your Mind,* read the chapter entitled "Accepting the Unacceptable." What meant the most to you from this chapter or helped you to think more accurately about God's character and the truth of His Word?

What offered you the greatest challenge or blessing, and why?

A Problem

How do you generally handle shocking news or an unfair situation?

What would those closest to you say about your ability to face your problems or accept change?

A Scripture

Write out Romans 11:33 from the Bible version you use.

Next write out any problems or issues you are dealing with, either present or past.

Lay your problems next to the forever-truths of Romans 11:33.

What do you learn about your problems?

What do you learn about God?

An Instrument

Have you memorized Romans 11:33? Why not do it now?

Look at Psalm 119:9 and 11. What are the benefits of memorizing Scripture?

What reigning position should God's Word have in your life, according to Colossians 3:16?

How did Jesus handle temptation in Matthew 4:4, 7, and 10?

How could having Romans 11:33 hidden in your heart become a mighty instrument in God's hands to help you with all your problems?

An Acceptance

Think again of your most pressing problem or the most unexplainable event in your life. Then pray through Romans 11:33, and check each of the attitudes below that indicate your "acceptance of the unacceptable"—your acceptance of God's will and way for your life.

__ I don't have to understand everything.

__ I don't need to understand everything.

__ I can't understand everything.

__ Why ask "Why"?

__ It's O.K.

__ Let it go.

__ Let God be God.

__ Let go of your right to know.

__ These are God's judgments.

__ These are God's ways.

__ No vengeance!

__ It's not them, it's Him!

Spend some added time in prayer about the attitudes you are unable to check. Ask God to continue to teach you to love Him with all your mind. Also ask Him to help you let go of those things about your life that you don't understand. And thank Him for all He has taught you in this study of six powerful passages from His Word!

Loving God...Even More

Read this section in your book again. As you consider the contents of this chapter and God's amazing love for you, what can you do this week, in obedience to Christ...

...to think on the truth about God?

...to trust God "in the dark"?

...to love God with all your mind?

Oh what a wonderful God we have!

*L*EADING A BIBLE STUDY DISCUSSION GROUP

༼ ᎗

*W*hat a privilege it is to lead a Bible study! And what joy and excitement await you as you delve into the Word of God and help others to discover its life-changing truths. If God has called you to lead a Bible study group, I know you'll be spending much time in prayer and planning and giving much thought to being an effective leader. I also know that taking the time to read through the following tips will help you navigate the challenges of leading a Bible study discussion group and enjoy the effort and opportunity.

The Leader's Roles

As a Bible study group leader, you'll find your role changing back and forth from *leader* to *cheerleader* to *lover* to *referee* during the course of a session.

Since you're the leader, group members will look to you to be the *leader* guiding them through the material. So be well prepared. In fact, be over-prepared so that you know the material better than any group member does. Start your study early in the week and let its message simmer all week long. (You might even work several lessons ahead so that you have in mind the big picture and the overall direction of the study.) Be ready to share some additional gems that your group members wouldn't have discovered on their own. That extra insight from your study time—or that comment from a wise Bible teacher or scholar, that clever saying, that keen observation from another believer, and even an appropriate joke—adds an element of fun and keeps Bible study from becoming routine, monotonous, and dry.

Next, be ready to be the group's *cheerleader.* Your energy and enthusiasm for the task at hand can be contagious. It can also stimulate people to get more involved in their personal study as well as in the group discussion.

Third, be the *lover,* the one who shows a genuine concern for the members of the group. You're the one who will establish the atmosphere of the group. If you laugh and have fun, the group members will laugh and have fun. If you hug, they will hug. If you care, they will care. If you share, they will share. If you love, they will love. So pray every day to love the women God has placed in your group. Ask Him to show you how to love them with His love.

Finally, as the leader, you'll need to be the *referee* on occasion. That means making sure everyone has an equal opportunity to speak. That's easier to do when you operate under the assumption that every member of the group has something worthwhile to contribute. So, trusting that the Lord has taught each person during the week, act on that assumption.

Leader, cheerleader, lover, and referee—these four roles of the leader may make the task seem overwhelming. But that's not bad if it keeps you on your knees praying for your group.

A Good Start

Beginning on time, greeting people warmly, and opening in prayer gets the study off to a good start. Know what you want to have happen during your time together and make sure those things get done. That kind of order means comfort for those involved.

Establish a format and let the group members know what that format is. People appreciate being in a Bible study that focuses on the Bible. So keep the discussion on the topic and move the group through the questions. Tangents are often hard to avoid—and even harder to rein in. So be sure to focus on the answers to questions about the specific passage at hand. After all, the purpose of the group is Bible study!

Finally, as someone has accurately observed, "Personal growth is one of the by-products of any effective small group. This growth is achieved when people are recognized and accepted by others. The more friendliness, mutual trust, respect, and warmth exhibited, the more likely that the member will find pleasure in the group, and, too, the more likely she will work hard toward the accomplishment of the group's goals. The effective leader will strive to reinforce desirable traits" (source unknown).

A Dozen Helpful Tips

Here is a list of helpful suggestions for leading a Bible study discussion group:

1. Arrive early, ready to focus fully on others and give of yourself. If you have to do any last-minute preparation, review, re-grouping, or praying, do it in the car. Don't dash in, breathless, harried, late, still tweaking your plans.

2. Check out your meeting place in advance. Do you have everything you need—tables, enough chairs, a blackboard, hymnals if you plan to sing, coffee, etc.?

3. Greet each person warmly by name as she arrives. After all, you've been praying for these women all week long, so let each VIP know that you're glad she's arrived.

4. Use name tags for at least the first two or three weeks.

5. Start on time no matter what—even if only one person is there!

6. Develop a pleasant but firm opening statement. You might say, "This lesson was great! Let's get started so we can enjoy all of it!" or "Let's pray before we begin our lesson."

7. Read the questions, but don't hesitate to reword them on occasion. Rather than reading an entire paragraph of instructions, for instance, you might say, "Question 1 asks us to list some ways that Christ displayed humility. Lisa, please share one way Christ displayed humility."

8. Summarize or paraphrase the answers given. Doing so will keep the discussion focused on the topic, eliminate digressions, help avoid or clear up any misunderstandings of the text, and keep each group member aware of what the others are saying.

9. Keep moving and don't add any of your own questions to the discussion time. It's important to get through the study guide questions. So if a cut-and-dried answer is called for, you don't need to comment with anything other than a "thank you." But when the question asks for an opinion or an application (for instance, "How can this truth help us in our marriages?" or "How do *you* find time for your quiet time?"), let all who want to contribute do so.

10. Affirm each person who contributes, especially if the contribution was very personal, painful to share, or a

quiet person's rare statement. Acknowledge everyone who shares a hero by saying something like "Thank you for sharing that insight from your own life" or "We certainly appreciate what God has taught you. Thank you for letting us in on it."

11. Watch your watch, put a clock right in front of you, or consider using a timer. Pace the discussion so that you meet your cut-off time, especially if you want time to pray. Stop at the designated time even if you haven't finished the lesson. Remember that everyone has worked through the study once; you are simply going over it again.

12. End on time. You can only make friends with your group members by ending on time or even a little early! Besides, members of your group have the next item on their agenda to attend to—picking up children from the nursery, babysitter, or school; heading home to tend to matters there; running errands; getting to bed; or spending some time with their husbands. So let them out *on time!*

Five Common Problems

In any group, you can anticipate certain problems. Here are some common ones that can arise, along with helpful solutions:

1. *The incomplete lesson*—Right from the start, establish the policy that if someone has not done the lesson, it is best for her not to answer the questions. But do try to include her responses to questions that ask for opinions or experiences. Everyone can share some thoughts in reply to a question like "Reflect on what you know about both athletic and spiritual training, and then share

what you consider to be the essential elements of training oneself in godliness."

2. *The gossip*—The Bible clearly states that gossiping is wrong, so you don't want to allow it in your group. Set a high and strict standard by saying, "I am not comfortable with this conversation," or "We [not *you*] are gossiping, ladies. Let's move on."

3. *The talkative member*—Here are three scenarios and some possible solutions for each.

   a. The problem talker may be talking because she has done her homework and is excited about something she has to share. She may also know more about the subject than the others and, if you cut her off, the rest of the group may suffer.

   SOLUTION: Respond with a comment like: "Sarah, you are making very valuable contributions. Let's see if we can get some reactions from the others," or "I know Sarah can answer this. She's really done her homework. How about some of the rest of you?"

   b. The talkative member may be talking because she has *not* done her homework and wants to contribute, but she has no boundaries.

   SOLUTION: Establish at the first meeting that those who have not done the lesson do not contribute except on opinion or application questions. You may need to repeat this guideline at the beginning of each session.

   c. The talkative member may want to be heard whether or not she has anything worthwhile to contribute.

SOLUTION: After subtle reminders, be more direct, saying, "Betty, I know you would like to share your ideas, but let's give others a chance. I'll call on you later."

4. *The quiet member*—Here are two scenarios and possible solutions.

a. The quiet member wants the floor but somehow can't get the chance to share.

SOLUTION: Clear the path for the quiet member by first watching for clues that she wants to speak (moving to the edge of her seat, looking as if she wants to speak, perhaps even starting to say something) and then saying, "Just a second. I think Chris wants to say something." Then, of course, make her a hero!

b. The quiet member simply doesn't want the floor.

SOLUTION: "Chris, what answer do you have on question 2?" or "Chris, what do you think about…?" Usually after a shy person has contributed a few times, she will become more confident and more ready to share. Your role is to provide an opportunity where there is *no* risk of a wrong answer. But occasionally a group member will tell you that she would rather not be called on. Honor her request, but from time to time ask her privately if she feels ready to contribute to the group discussions.

In fact, give all your group members the right to pass. During your first meeting, explain that any time a group member does not care to share an answer, she may simply say, "I pass." You'll want to repeat this policy at the beginning of every group session.

5. *The wrong answer*—Never tell a group member that she has given a wrong answer, but at the same time never let a wrong answer go by.

> SOLUTION: Either ask if someone else has a different answer or ask additional questions that will cause the right answer to emerge. As the women get closer to the right answer, say, "We're getting warmer! Keep thinking! We're almost there!"

Learning from Experience

Immediately after each Bible study session, evaluate the group discussion time using this checklist. You may also want a member of your group (or an assistant or trainee or outside observer) to evaluate you periodically.

May God strengthen—and encourage!—you as you assist others in the discovery of His many wonderful truths.

About the Author

Elizabeth George is a bestselling author who has more than 4.8 million books in print. She is a popular speaker at Christian women's events. Her passion is to teach the Bible in a way that changes women's lives. For information about Elizabeth's speaking ministry, to sign up for her mailings, or to purchase her books visit her website:

www.ElizabethGeorge.com

Books by Elizabeth George

...tiful in God's Eyes

Finding God's Path Through Your Trials

- Following God with All Your Heart
- Life Management for Busy Women
- Loving God with All Your Mind
- A Mom After God's Own Heart
- Powerful Promises for Every Woman
- The Remarkable Women of the Bible
- Small Changes for a Better Life
- Walking with the Women of the Bible
- A Wife After God's Own Heart
- A Woman After God's Own Heart®
- A Woman After God's Own Heart® Deluxe Edition
- A Woman After God's Own Heart®—A Daily Devotional
- A Woman After God's Own Heart® Collection
- A Woman's Call to Prayer
- A Woman's High Calling
- A Woman's Walk with God
- A Young Woman After God's Own Heart
- A Young Woman After God's Own Heart—A Devotional
- A Young Woman's Call to Prayer
- A Young Woman's Walk with God

Study Guides

- Beautiful in God's Eyes Growth & Study Guide
- Finding God's Path Through Your Trials Growth & Study Guide
- Following God with All Your Heart Growth & Study Guide
- Life Management for Busy Women Growth & Study Guide
- Loving God with All Your Mind Growth & Study Guide
- A Mom After God's Own Heart Growth & Study Guide
- The Remarkable Women of the Bible Growth & Study Guide
- Small Changes for a Better Life Growth & Study Guide
- Understanding Your Blessings in Christ
- A Wife After God's Own Heart Growth & Study Guide
- A Woman After God's Own Heart® Growth & Study Guide
- A Woman's Call to Prayer Growth & Study Guide
- A Woman's High Calling Growth & Study Guide
- A Woman's Walk with God Growth & Study Guide

Children's Books

- God's Wisdom for Little Girls
- A Little Girl After God's Own Heart

Books by Jim & Elizabeth George

- God Loves His Precious Children
- God's Wisdom for Little Boys
- A Little Boy After God's Own Heart

Books by Jim George

- The Bare Bones Bible® Handbook
- The Bare Bones Bible® Bios
- A Husband After God's Own Heart
- A Man After God's Own Heart
- The Remarkable Prayers of the Bible
- A Young Man After God's Own Heart

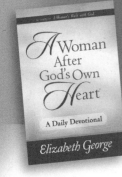

STUDIES *for* BUSY WOMEN